50 Years

A Poetical Memoir

GW00776608

Barry Firman

A CIP catalogue record for this book is available
from the British Library

ISBN 978-1-916703-04-9

Typeset by Eleanor Baggaley
First Published 2023 by Snowdrop Publishing
www.Snowdrop-Publishing.com

Acknowledgements

I would like to thank all of the people who got me to where I am today and for their encouragement to bring all of my poems together in this book.

My family, of course, my wife Linda who has been by my side for almost 50 years and all of my work colleagues throughout my entire career. I have made lots of friends whilst working on the buses, passengers included. Thank you for the fun times and inspiration.

The stories I have collected and material for the poems have nearly all come from my time as a bus conductor and driver and I have enjoyed my time working for Stagecoach and still do to this day.

I would also like to thank Eleanor Baggaley for all her help enabling me to complete this book as I didn't have a clue where to start. She guided me through the process with her professional expertise and knowledge.

Contents

Introduction

Now I'm coming up to 50 years on the buses, I have collected lots of stories over that time. As well as my hobby of writing poetry and comic verse, lots of people have said I should write a book. So here it is.

I think I had better start with a little introduction of my early life and how I came to start working on the buses.

I was born Barry Edward Firman on the 9th of July 1955 to George and Catherine Firman. I was the 6th child and at the time we were living in Tarset Street in Byker. I was found to have a hole in the heart which resulted in my family being able to quickly move to a cleaner area of the city, North Kenton.

My early school years were spent at Pendower Hall Open Air school which catered for children with a variety of disabilities. I stayed there until the age of 11 when my dad was told I could attend mainstream school and I moved to Kenton Comprehensive. When I first went to Kenton school I was put in the middle of the education grades because Pendower concentrated more on health and basic education but I'm pleased to say that over the next couple of years, I went up in the grades until I left in 1970, aged 15.

My younger brother came into the family 6 years after me resulting in 3 boys and 4 girls. Home life was quite good being 1 of 7; Georgina, Richard, Geraldine, Carole, Patricia, Barry and Kevin.

Sadly when I was 8 years old our mother passed away from cancer but Dad and my older siblings took care of us. Dad worked nights at the shipyards and would do anything to make a bit of money. On his way home in the morning, he would pick up any bits of scrap he saw lying about so he could eventually take them to Shepherd's scrap merchants for cash.

One night he told me he was keeping me off school the next day to help him. I didn't realise he had borrowed a horse and cart from someone he knew, we loaded it up and set off at 8.30 in the morning to the scrap merchants just when a lot of my school friends were passing. So at the age of 14, I endured weeks of being labelled 'Steptoe and Son.'

Another money-making scheme of his was every night he went to work with a suitcase, haversack and large shopping bag all filled with cigarettes, sweets, biscuits, pop and various other items, which he would sell to his workmates at

break times. As I said, any way to make mone͜
do it and it all went to feeding and clothing the ͺ
he always had my full respect, however, we did haν
differences as I got older and I left home at the age of 16
live with my sister Carole.

When I left school I first got a job as a commie waiter
at Gosforth Park Hotel. I liked that job and I have always
enjoyed working with people. After about 2 years I left to
work in the Swallow Hotel in Newcastle. I was only there for
3 months because of numerous disagreements with a certain
Head waiter and I lost my temper which resulted in me
getting sacked. After a short spell on the dole, I got a job
as a sheet metal worker, which I hated and 9 months later
packed that in and started on the buses. I should mention
that while I was living with my sister, her husband Rob was
a bus driver at Slatyford depot and said to me, 'You won't
last,' but here I am 48 years later. Cheers, Rob.

While Rob was working on the buses one day a rather
large lady came to board his bus. Now in those days, the
doors had a grab pole in the middle to help people step onto
the bus. Rob said to the lady, 'Both sides please,' with a
wink and the lady just called him a cheeky bugger and got
on. When Rob finished his shift and went home, who was
sitting in his house but the large lady who just happened to
be our aunty Sylvia. She then said, 'That's him, that's the
cheeky bugger!' glad to say they had a good laugh about it.

As you read the book, there is a little Geordie slang. If you're not from the North East, here's a guide for some of the words you will come across.

Bait - lunch or a snack

Gowk - a fool or someone being awkward

Wor lass - my girl/ girlfriend/ wife

Toon - town, of course!

Chapter 1

Dad

A couple of years ago Nationwide Building Society did a few adverts on saving money which gave me an idea for the first short poem about my dad.

I once asked my dad about opening his shop at break time from work and he told me that a long time ago, on his way home after a night shift, a couple of other work colleagues asked him to bring a packet of tabs or a bottle of pop when he came back that night. He saw an opportunity to make a little bit extra and so started the idea of taking all that he did into work and selling at break times, he used to often take me shopping with him when he bought all the multipacks of biscuits, etc. and I thought they were for the house, alas no.

Nationwide

Where were you when my mum died?

My dad had not a penny,
That he could save,
Seven children, money had,
He just waved...

Goodbye.
God knows he tried.

Every night he went to work,
With the corner shop,
With cigarettes and biscuits,
And bottles of pop.

On his way home in the morning,
Pick up bits of scrap,
Like bicycle wheels,
Or a broken tap.

Then when he had a lot,
Off to Shepherds we'd go,
Get it weighed then paid,
And home once more.

Green shield stamps, Co-op dividend books,
Anything able,
That helped to buy clothes,
And put food on the table.

So I'm sorry Nationwide,
If my dad didn't bother,
Cos what he had came in one hand,
And out of the other.

    I must admit we didn't go short of food. He was a good cook; he served his time in the army as a cook and we always joked that he made enough to feed the street. In a way, it was true because I was often sent across to my aunt's house and sometimes along to a lady whom my dad was friendly with, with a bag containing a couple of dinners, a tin of gravy and anything extra he had left.

Chapter 2

1974

On the 28th of January 1974, I started life as a conductor following the initial training at Byker depot. I went to Slatyford and was put with a gentleman called John Vietch to continue my training.

There are quite a few characters mentioned throughout my time on the buses and John was a nice fellow with a wicked sense of humour and would think nothing of starting an argument in the canteen and then quietly melting into the background to watch the fun play out.

I started paired with a driver called Frankie Duers. It didn't last long as he wanted to be with his girlfriend, Kitty Banks, so I moved on to work with a lovely man called John Davison because his conductress, Dot Avery was moving to work in the office.

And so started a great time with John for the next 2 to 3 years. He would regularly get me to run into the betting shop and put his bets on as we passed by and then next time around nip in and get his winnings. Bait times were sometimes spent in the pub rather than the canteen; not really allowed but who knew?

Now it was around this time in 1974 that Newcastle United had reached the FA Cup final against Liverpool and on that Saturday I was working at West Walls sub depot with a gentleman called Tommy Straker. When it got to about 2 o'clock he said I could, 'get off home,' if I wanted to so I could watch the match. I told him I would stay and watch it here as we only had a black and white TV at home and the depot had colour TVs. Sad to say we got beaten 3-0 and a certain Kevin Keegan ran the show.

I was once talking about a new girlfriend and I referred to her as, 'wor lass,' well John went mad. He didn't think I should talk like that about her until we were married so I agreed and as it happened that certain young lady became my wife, or wor lass, sorry John.

In 1975 British Leyland went on strike for a very long time and as TWPTE had a lot of Leyland Atlanteans, we were running out of parts to repair the vehicles. A request was sent to other bus companies to borrow whatever vehicles they could spare. Two very old backenders were loaned to

Byker from Leeds and the 64 route was shared by Byker and Slatyford. John and I were on a bait stop at Byker and were walking to the pick-up point at Chillingham Road when I saw one of these vehicles waiting for us. Well, John burst out laughing and said, 'You're going to do some work today,' and he was right. With an old vehicle like that, the bells were 1 for stop, 2 for go, 3 for emergency stop, and 4 for full. When I noticed someone getting off, I'd ring the bell just as someone else also rang it, just as well I had a very good driver in John who knew what was happening and kept an eye on things.

I had some really good times with John and became friends with his sons and his lovely wife Nora but sadly one day I went to work at the Haymarket sub depot and John was playing cards. He kept dropping them, we noticed something wasn't right and immediately sent for an ambulance. Two drivers carried him downstairs and I found out later that John had had a stroke and that was our time as driver and mate finished.

I spent the next couple of years with various drivers including Davy Stoker. Davy was a tall skinny lad who could handle himself no problem and got into many a scrape, to put it mildly, especially on one occasion when I was having trouble getting a youth to pay his fare. I managed to eventually get his fare out of him but when I came downstairs Davy wanted to know why I had been so long. When I told him, he asked me to point the lad out. I didn't need to as when we got to Eldon Square, the lad came down and started banging the used ticket box to which Davy said, 'Whoa man have you got no toys at home?' Well the kid must have thought Davy was small like me because he sat low in the cab and threatened Davy to get off the bus, 'and he would have him.' Oops! Davy got out of the cab and the lad seeing his size panicked and searched for the emergency handle at the centre doors. By this time, Davy was outside the doors and grabbed the lad, left him on the ground, got back on the bus and continued with the journey. It was about this time I decided to go for driver training; my first attempt was awful. After only three days I came out of the driving school and the instructor who was only about 2 inches taller than me told me to get in the cab after some big six-foot-plus driver had just got out and said, 'Can you reach the pedals?'

I said, 'No,' while my legs were just swinging away.

'Well, we have a lot of vehicles like this.'

I said 'They all have this, the seat winds down,' but I knew he didn't think I'd make it so I quit, albeit temporarily.

When I was on with John and I met my future wife, there was a disco every Thursday night at the PTE club and in late October 1974 I went along with my sister and friend George.

It was on this night that George and I asked two young girls to dance and arranged to meet them a couple of nights later. The two young ladies were Linda and Heather Jackson.

Linda told me that as she worked on Stanhope Street she got to know a lot of the conductors on the 39 and 40 routes and they had invited her to come to the disco. This worked to my advantage as we got on so well that a couple of years later, on the 9th of July 1977, we got married. And 45 years later it is still one of the best things that ever happened to me.

Now as I was saying about characters on the buses there were a couple of stories that I love about the time we were conductors. In particular, a driver called Roy and his conductor, Chris on one occasion were travelling up Deckham Bank and found a large steering wheel at the side of the road. Roy put it in the cab beside him, on the return journey back down the bank Chris was busy taking fares when Roy picked up the steering wheel held it out of the cab and shouted, 'Chris, look what's happened!' Well, Chris playing along with the joke just screamed, as did one or two passengers.

I never did find out what happened after that but it made for a really good laugh in the depot at the time. On another occasion, one of the termini was at Fewster Square where there was a swimming pool, so Chris and Roy decided that as they had a good amount of time at this terminus they would go in for a swim. The next day they brought swimming trunks and towels and went in the pool. When they came out, not realising how long they had been in they were very late so they blanked the screens and flew to Newcastle and came back on service at Ridley Place.

On arriving there the inspector asked them, 'What RTC are you on?'

They said '9 Wrekenton,'

'Where's 6, 7 and 8?' The inspector said, 'They should be in front of you but because of an accident on Pilgrim Street everything is being held up.'

Roy's quick reply was, 'When we came over the bridge a policeman stopped us and diverted us so we just came on here.' Talk about quick thinking, to me that was excellent.

Now when I mentioned me and John going to the pub on our bait time, it was nothing new to be doing then as you would find lots of crews (drivers and conductors) in the Three Bulls or the Farmers Rest. It was accepted then and was not unheard of to be sitting in there when you were supposed to be 'spare' upstairs. It's not now, oh how times have changed.

Another great character about that time was Neville Fail. Now for anyone who knew Neville, he was the ultimate conductor. Nobody got off with a fare and the bus was never early. Smartly dressed, (Sargent Major was his nickname) he would regularly get off the bus at the toilets at Gallowgate and wait until the bus was on time before getting back on and quite a few times he was left there as the driver knew what he was doing and wanted to get off at Eldon Square for his bait. On his days off you would see him at the corner by the Rokerby pub, now a Farm Foods, on Stamfordham Road staring at his watch and checking who was running early. The number of times he applied for inspector would have been a record but the powers that be couldn't make him one because we'd have nobody left on the job.

By 1978, I was married and looking to progress so I went back to driving school. After three weeks I took my test and passed so there was no stopping me then and I never looked back. Not long after that, the company went through the process of making all the routes a one-man operation, getting rid of all the conductors. It took a few years for this to happen with us all saying the 60s would not go to being 'one-man,' but they did and eventually, the 39 and 40s did too.

Sadly when we lost all the conductors, that meant Neville had to leave. He died a few years later, being laid to rest in his favourite place, the English Martyrs church. Neville wasn't the only one to be left at the last stop, I once told

John I was nipping into the toilets at the library only to come out and find John had forgotten and carried on. I caught the next bus up to Ridley Place to find him sitting there giggling saying he didn't realise I had got off. Another character that was on the buses during that time was a gentleman known as Dickie Bow. Not his real name but those on the job at the time will know who he is. A story went around that he was spotted in Ponteland dressed as a Frenchman with a bike and a string of onions around his neck so I wrote the next poem, which gave us all a laugh at the time.

When I first went driving I was paired with a young lad with bright ginger hair called, of all things, Kevin Orange. I struck up a great friendship with him and my wife and I regularly went out with Kevin and his wife, Pauline. In 1979 on the 7th of August, we had our first child Christopher and Kevin Orange was Christopher's godfather. We were living in a flat at the time and saving money by not going out as much. We decided to try and buy a house which we managed a few months later; a small semi-detached in Fenham. We lived there for about two years before moving up to Chapel House where we've been ever since.

Getting back to the job, I was doing quite well as the Metro was being built and our wages were kept in line with whatever was happening on the Metro. I also progressed to being a one-man operation so things were looking up.

Dickie Bow

Thought I'd tell you a story,
Of a colleague who was not shy,
He'd come to work in full uniform,
But wearing a dickie bow tie.

They say he once dressed as a Frenchman,
Now this is a tale you might like,
Was seen riding around Ponteland,
With onions, French beret, and a bike.

So he knocked on a door in the village,
Being sure as a Frenchman he'd pass,
Then said 'Avez vous un cuppa?'
And followed with, 'Ta bonny lass,'

The lady was quite puzzled by this,
It's not what a Frenchman would say,
And as she spoke the language fluent,
Replied in French, 'Yes it's quite a nice day,'

Well Dickie Bow stood in amazement,
And didn't know quite what to do,
Bonjour, Bonsoir and Escargo,
Was the only French that he knew,

So he quickly ran down the garden,
And thought he'd best take a hike,
He hopped it as fast as his frog legs would go,
Cos Madam is keeping his bike.

Chapter 3

Tall Ships

In the mid-1980s a great event happened in Newcastle; The Tall Ships arrived on the Tyne it was great. The route I was driving at the time went down to the quayside and passed all these magnificent vessels that were docked. The crowds of people that came to see them were overwhelming, making it a very busy time indeed but I didn't mind as I got to witness this great event every day. They have been back a couple of times since but recently they seem to be at Hartlepool Marina. It's not too far away and still great for the North East.

In 1986 the Conservative government, led by Margaret Thatcher deregulated public services so things like the PTE (Passenger Transport Executive) were no more. When deregulation happened, it was the worst time in my memory of the buses. Services changed so much that people didn't know what was happening and the company didn't have much of a clue either.

There were rumours about being taken over by various companies. At the time, we were in competition with Tyne and Wear Omnibus Company (TWOC). The tricks that both sides used would not be allowed today; waiting at the bus stop until the competition arrived and picking up as many passengers as you could so as not to leave him any at all.

Time boards didn't seem to matter as long as the work was done, messages would come over the radio telling you where the competition was, and a lot of the drivers working for the competition were drivers who had taken redundancy from us. It seemed like they were then trying to put us out of business, so there was no love lost in putting them out of business instead. The same thing happened again a little later when Welcome came onto the scene, and after that HMB although by the time the last one arrived, we were growing a little tired of doing everything we could to help the company get rid of the competition only to find the company did not repay the favour.

About this time the poetic juices were flowing and I came up with one or two about the competition we were facing.

It's Only A Game

There's a new game out at the moment,
Played by buses both sides of the city,
Against a company best known as Welcome,
Who are surviving too long, more's the pity.

You don't need a board to play this game,
Or a computer with a joystick or mouse,
You just need a bus and a driver,
And a route say Wallsend - Chapel House.

The aim is to pick up the most passengers,
You can do this by fair or foul means,
The winner is the one who can get the most on,
Till they resemble a tin of sardines.

There are all sorts of ways to achieve this,
And so many strokes you can pull,
Like going past stops almost empty,
Cos you know the next one will be full.

And when you arrive at St James',
Wait and wait till your passengers frown,
When Welcome appears right behind you,
Go like the wind right into town.

It's not just our drivers that do this,
They can also pull a few tricks,
But what can you expect from their drivers,
They used to do it here too, mud sticks.

Sometimes the Welcome goes missing,
And you're wondering, 'Where can he be?'
Then a voice comes over the radio,
'Who's looking for 373?'

He's been spotted down on the by-pass,
So there's no reason now you should wait,
He's got no one on and showing blanks,
And he's flying to town for his bait.

The latest trick I've seen from Welcome,
Happened three times the other day,
He reversed into the street just beside me,
And left Chapel House the wrong way.

Now I hope no one takes me too seriously,
Or I may end up with a visit,
Then I'd have to explain what I mean,
When I say, 'It's only a game isn't it?'

It's fair to say when HMB came along, that the best thing that came out of fighting off the competition was that the attitude of most of the drivers changed for the better. Before all this, it was just a job and passengers were there to be picked up and that was that. After this, we realised that if it weren't for the passengers we wouldn't have a job so we began to interact a little, 'Hello, good morning,' and, 'Thank you,' helped build a relationship with the passengers. I know you can't please everyone but if you're seen to be trying it goes a long way.

By 1989 we became Busways Travel Services on an Employee Share Ownership Plan (ESOP). I had been very close to looking for another job. Like I said most drivers were getting a bit fed up with doing everything we could to help the company out only for it all to be forgotten afterwards. We did our jobs and left it all to management to put duplicates out. Eventually, they bought out the competition to get rid of them, then laws were passed which put an end to it all anyway. Things improved following the takeover and we felt as though we might as well stay. After all, I had a mortgage and a young family to think of and changing jobs seemed a bit risky.

One such company to run in competition with us for a while was Andersons which inspired me to write this next piece. Some may notice it's to the tune of *The Ballad of John and Yoko*.

The Ballad of Busways

Standing at the Co-op this morning,
Waiting for the Anderson to show,
The man in the black said, 'You could get the sack,
You shouldn't even be here you know,'

Christ you know it ain't easy,
You know how hard it can be,
You can't do anything right,
To please this bloody company.

Blackett Street is getting ridiculous,
Sometimes nothing moving at all,
It just takes one gowk,
To leave his back sticking out,
And cause buses to line up wall-to-wall.

Christ you know it ain't easy,
You know how hard it can be,
One day we'll be stuck there,
From 12 o'clock till half past 3.

When you think today will be different,
You break down and it's right on the bend,
The fumes make you choke,
The radios broke,

Either that or Tommy's on the other end.

Christ you know it ain't easy,
But how we supposed to tell,
When he's on the radio,
He's like Scarlett Pimpernel.

The bosses say I part own the company,
Is that a steering wheel, a seat and cab light?
They're not the crown jewels,
And if I stick by the rules,
Will they let me take them home every night?

Christ you know it ain't easy,
You know how hard it can be,
I wish I could win the pools,
Then they could stick their company.

It was now about this time that pensioners were going to be charged a small amount per journey while some were up in arms about it a lot of pensioners didn't mind as it was only 15p.

15p

Well, now the time has come,
I thought I'd never see the day,
And though it's only 15p,
Still, the pensioners have to pay.

Amid the cries of, 'terrible,' and,
'Isn't it bloody scandalous?'
'They're charging us 3 shillings,
Just to ride upon their bus.'

3 bob in my day was a good night out,
At the pictures, 20 players with tips,
A taxi ride to get you home,
And change for fish and chips.

Now some old people don't mind the fare,
Will be ready without a word,
But some have said they'll be awkward,
The methods they'll use are absurd.

They'll all get on with fivers,
In the hope our change will go.
But we've got that sussed we'll give a receipt,
And tell them, 'change is at depot.'

While it's easier for us if they don't pay,
Our patience will start to abate,
If their methods cause constant delays,
Other people will just have to wait.

If they think they're hard done by in Newcastle,
Look at places like Blyth and Pegswood.
A few quid in tokens paid once a year,
Whey, they still never had it so good.

From the moment we became Busways we endured endless stories about being bought out by various other companies, one being Delta Transport, which prompted me to write this next short poem.

Delta

There's a story going around at the depot,
That Busways was being bought out,
By a company, they call Delta Transport,
And our bosses faced being kicked out.

The drivers would all get lump sums,
And new contracts to houses be sent,
Reports that the cash could be thousands,
My wife would still have it all spent.

Though it's not known who started the story,
One man has been blamed for the rumour,
Poor Topsy was named as the culprit,
And now he's lost all sense of humour.

For when management heard, they called Topsy,
And said if more stories came back,
To damage the name of the company,
'I'm afraid you'll be facing the sack.'

Now Topsy has said if he hears,
Anyone mention buyout or Delta,
He won't get the sack for a story,
He'll thump them and go with a belta.

Chapter 4

The 1990s

A few things happened in the early 1990s. I will start with the riots that happened in most major cities in 1991. It all began in Newcastle, starting with Meadowell and later spreading to Benwell and Scotswood. As with most disturbances, it was mainly youths who were responsible for setting fire to houses, cars, etc. and the burning down of a pub, The Dodds Arms, on Elswick Road. They were worrying times for buses because we dared not go near the areas affected, especially at night.

The Riots, September 1991

Is it the youth that's gone wild, looting and burning,
In the hands of a child, are the weapons for turning,
A street once so peaceful, in an area quiet,
A Molotov cocktail, the spark of a riot.

They gather on corners, at dusk after school,
Strength among numbers, with fear the mob rule,
It's not anger or boredom when violence is loose,
They just look for a reason, a feeble excuse.

This time it's because two idiots crashed,
Joyriders, criminals lost their lives in a smash,
Stole someone's car, lost control, hit a post,
Burst into flames and cooked them like toast.

In North Sheilds, they rioted, just as night fell,
It happened in Scotswood, Cowgate and Benwell,
They burnt down the Dodds and the Robin Adair,
Set empty houses on fire without a care.

Throw bricks at police and the fire brigade,
Then watch on TV, the damage they've made,
They think they're all great, it's a laugh it's a lark,
Causing mayhem and fear, roaming streets after dark.

When it's all settled down the MPs will say,
'We need money and jobs in this area today,'
People around here do not get enough,
My answer to all the do-gooders is, 'TOUGH.'

This next poem was inspired by some interesting driving
I witnessed. It should probably come with a trigger warn-
ing given the conclusion of the poem from some dangerous
driving.

Charlie

When Charlie was born he was the first,
To the Smiths who were fit to burst,
But little did they know what he'd bring,
As he grew up, he was first at everything.

The first one at school every day,
First in the yard when they went out to play,
Top of the class in every test,
Yes, Charlie knew he was the best.

Then when Charles turned 17,
He realised a lifelong dream,
To drive a car, he'd be the best,
Especially passing his driving test *(1st time)*.

Overtaking, across lanes he flew,
Just to be the first in the queue,
Doesn't matter if it's day or night,
First to roundabouts and traffic lights.

Alas poor Charles, out of luck,
Overtook on a bend, not seeing the truck.
Couldn't stop, he was going too fast,
Now Charles the first, he breathed his last.

On the 5th of April 1993, my father died aged 71 after a long fight with bowel cancer, which he kept from most of the family until near the end. Looking back I wish I had been a more loving son; we had our differences but I can only say the way he brought us all up after our mother died earned huge respect from me. End of an era, RIP George William Firman.

Dad

Father died the 5th of April,
Nineteen ninety three,
Stuck his tongue out, licked his lips,
Then passed on peacefully.

After everyone had seen him,
And said their last goodbyes,
We said thank you to the nurses,
Cleared our throats and dried our eyes.

Then made our way to my house,
To see what's to be done,
Talk about the past,
Tea and biscuits everyone.

The next day we met at Carole's flat,
To sort out his personal things,
Like photographs and watches,
His medals and his rings.

We knew we weren't rich,
He never had a lot of lolly,
He'd just bought himself a carpet,
And a brand new shopping trolly.

Now Dad told me a few weeks ago,
Of an heirloom the family had,
An ivory-handled clothes brush,
That came from his grandad.

He'd like someone to have it,
In our family, not theirs,
And as it was a Firman thing,
We're rightful sole and heirs.

So while sorting his possessions,
We thought, someone's in luck,
Until we came across this treasure,
A Catalogue plastic duck.

Was this the family heirloom?
Surely it can't be,
Who wants this precious item?
We all said, 'No not me.'

Though Gerry said, 'I'll take it,
I can use it for the dog,'
And Carol said, 'If it was mine,
I'd use it for the bog.'

When Gina came we asked her,
Surely it's not what Dad meant,
Then Gina laughed and told us,
It's what a catalogue had sent.

Well so much for family treasure,
It seems we're out of luck,
With old photos, junk and a shopping trolly,
And a catalogue plastic duck!

On the 20th of March 1994, we celebrated the birth of our second son, Jordan Edward George Firman. You may notice nearly 15 years between the two boys but we lost a little girl at birth in between and decided not to have any more children. Imagine my surprise when at the age of 38 Linda told me she was pregnant. The shock and horror of starting again, but looking back the best thing that happened to us. He was always going to be Jordan but Edward was my middle name and George in memory of my late father.

Moving on to 1996 the inevitable happened, Busways were bought out by Stagecoach and as Busways was an ESOP, we all got a small amount of cash. This helped tremendously with having a young family once again. We were informed at the time that within 3 years every bus we drove would be no more than 3 years old and we fell for it. Someone asked what would happen if we did not accept it and we were told that Stagecoach would just move in nearby and put us out of business so we agreed, and to be honest it hasn't turned out too bad.

Chapter 5

Busways Summer Outing

Just like any large company, we had summer outings and winter pantomimes organised by the welfare society and they did a very good job. A driver, Derek Thompson, regularly organised trips to other depots for nights out of indoor games, quizzes, green bowls, etc. We had some great times at these places with lots of friendly banter between the drivers. The summer outings included trips to Flamingo Land or Lightwater Valley with a lot of buses being driven by any driver who was willing to do it.

Busways Summer Outing

They boarded up the cafes,
And the car parks closed till noon,
From Newcastle to Yorkshire,
On Sunday 10th of June.

The reason for this action,
For anyone who's doubting,
Is just standard procedure,
For a Busways summer outing.

The weather wasn't bad this year,
A little cold but fine,
What should have been 8.30 prompt,
Was more like 5 to 9.

Meet up at the Odeon,
That seemed to be the ploy,
Fill each bus, leave no one out,
Then go in a convoy.

Destination Flamingo Land,
Last year went off great,
But got as far as Gateshead,
And again we had to wait.

Arrived 11.30,
After stopping at some town,
A tea and toilet break they said,
But the cafes were closed down.

Be back at 6 they said again,
The moment we arrived,
Then searched us out to tell us,
We were leaving there at 5.

We asked the reason for the change,
Our questions went unheard,
It was still after 6 when we left,
The whole thing was absurd.

But made sense to us later,
When driving like Brands Hatch,
The men were in a hurry,
To get back for the match.

The trip this year was organised,
By chairman of the board,
Mr seen it, had it, won it,
Done everything, (Sir) Norman Ward.

Helped at times by Diesel Don,
Busways' Chubby Brown,
Whose loud and bawdy manner,
Is known all over town.

A good day out was had by all,
On rides that made us sick,
No toilet stops going back,
We made it double-quick.

A thought for next year's outing,
Pick a place to stay,
Where the kids can all enjoy it,
And the men won't rush away.

When Stagecoach took over this all stopped, as they wouldn't allow the buses to be used and so the welfare society had to hire the buses and drivers which increased the cost. The theme parks didn't give much discount even though we could take over 300 people to the venue, this proved too much for the welfare society so they had to look elsewhere. We now go to Ocean Beach in South Shields which is still a good day out, as for the winter it's nearly always The Tyne Theatre for a pantomime. A great time is always guaranteed so well done to the welfare society for all the work you put in over the years.

As well as the welfare society, there were lots of activities where drivers got together and formed little groups. We've had pool teams competing in the local leagues, a rambling club where a few drivers used to go for a couple of days to the Lake District and other similar places. These days we have quite a few drivers who ride their bikes for miles and do quite a lot for charities. Every year they ride from Seahouses to Tynemouth raising a lot of money for the Chronicle Sunshine Fund and a few drivers also compete in the Great North Run.

The Slatyford Rambling Club

Come along and join us,
In the Slatyford Rambling Club,
Our walks go far and wide,
But always end up at a pub.

You can bring your wives and girlfriends,
As lots of others do,
We're a normal friendly bunch,
Except for one or two.

Like John's dog Fleck for instance,
If only to be fair,
His wife Moira sometimes comes,
But the dog is always there.

Then there's Kev 'The Belly,'
Never brings the girl he married,
He reckons with a gut like that,
He's got enough to carry.

We've even got the boss involved,
'Wor Ian' to the rest,
Who'll agree since he knows both depots,
Slatyford's the best.

Big John's lengthy strides,
Set off a cracking pace,
That seems to Stevie 'Little Legs,'
Like running in a race.

But when they get back to the bus,
His comments just the same,
'By wasn't that a good walk,
I could do it all again.'

But while most of us enjoy the view,
If speed is what you lack,
Some of us storm on ahead,
Kev Gunton brings the back.

We've done more miles than Byker,
Earned more for charities too,
But *they* always get the coverage,
In the old Busways news.

We have quite a lot of drivers who get dressed up at Christmas, Easter, and Halloween and a lot of money is donated to charities from collection buckets on the buses where the public has donated spare change. Of all the drivers that get dressed up, I feel I must mention a favourite of mine who every Christmas dresses as Widow Twanky. His costume and make-up are excellent and he has a great sense of humour to go with it. John Middlemass, not just fun at Christmas but at Easter collects eggs and books for the children of Hadrian School, a special education school and other good causes. If I go back a bit in time to the 80s, we had a driver called Jimmy Wilkinson, a rather large fellow with a jovial manner who looked just like Father Christmas. He didn't need to wear make-up or accessories, he already had a big white beard. He was a lovely man who I'm sorry to say died long before his time, another character who'll be missed by those who knew him.

Now as any driver will tell you it is quite an achievement to go a full year without a little mishap such as losing a mirror or a slight bump and hopefully nothing too serious but if you do then you are awarded a certificate and if you manage to continue to be accident-free for several years the awards get even better, and you are presented with these awards at the annual dinner dance.

Safe Driving Awards

I was worried just the other day,
I nearly had a crash,
Then I wouldn't get an invite,
To the annual Busways bash.

A dinner dance held every year,
Rewarding drivers' skill,
At missing cars and bus stops,
No accident forms to fill.

The food's not bad, the speeches drag,
And a disco ends the night,
But just when you think it's over,
You're guaranteed a fight.

Last year's main event,
Could top any boxing bill,
For in one corner stood Allan Gray,
Known as 'THE ANIMAL',

His opponent for the night,
He swears he wasn't drunk,
Was little Jimmy Ferry,
With turn-ups in his trunks.

But when they got together,
With one almighty roar,
A crowd stepped in to separate,
And called the match a draw.

This year we thought we'd made it,
And got down to the bus,
But Byker didn't send one,
Which caused an awful fuss.

There was language flying everywhere,
Some threw fists as well,
When someone tried to referee,
He was told to go to hell.

With chaos reigning everywhere,
It's Byker vs. Slaty,
And all this at a dance,
To reward the drivers' safety.

So you see why I was worried,
That I would miss my chance,
And wouldn't get an invite,
For the rematch at the dance.

As the years roll on and like any other business we ask for more wages and need newer buses and equipment so fares have to go up. When I started, it was 11p to the town, today it's £3.10 but a cost of living government cap is holding the fare at £2.00. It reminds me of a time the fares went up to 70p to the town and a lot of people were not happy.

Fares Fair

The fares have gone up once again,
70p to the town makes you think,
Though the rise isn't much,
only 3p or such,
And you'd pay twice that amount for a drink.

Of course, a lot of people won't pay that,
the 28 standard fare will be 30,
Whether beauties all dressed,
in their fine Sunday best,
Or the tramps that are scruffy and dirty.

Most people nowadays, they have passes,
the dates are a sight to behold,
If you manage to see,
I'll bet one out of three,
Is more than a week or two old.

Don't worry about that on your last trip,
if you get anything at all it's a plus,
Just be thankful that night,
there isn't a fight,
And you've still got some seats on the bus.

You could always radio assistance,
but sometimes you think, 'What's the use?'
By the time Police come,
troubles got off and run,
Leaving behind just threats and abuse.

When you try to explain that the increase,
isn't down to us getting more pay,
They just laugh and say,
'aye, and pigs might fly,'
'Well didn't bacon go up yesterday?'

Chapter 6

The Pigeon

Every bus driver must have a tale about experiences with animals—from fighting dogs to birds hitting the windscreens. I was reminded of a story about a driver, John Gray, who on getting to the terminus at Welbeck Road, got out of the bus and was eating an apple. Beside him was a horse tethered on the grass, John gave the apple to the horse and turned to get back on the bus. The horse followed him and also got on the bus. Try as he might, he could not get the horse off, he contacted control but they thought he was joking, I suppose he did eventually get it off and continue his journey but to this day, I have no idea how.

Like many drivers, I have come across stray horses wandering onto roads, cattle escaped from fields and the occasional stray dog wanting to get on the bus out of the rain.

One day I was paying in at the end of the shift when another driver, Sean, said he had a young lad ask him if he wanted to buy a pigeon. After a bit of a laugh Sean said to me, 'Barry, you could write a poem about it.'

The Pigeon

I thought I'd heard it all,
It's enough to make you cuss,
But a lad has beat them all tonight,
When he got on the bus.

'Do you want to buy a pigeon?
Sorry, it's not going cheap.'
'I cannot reach my money,
My arms are short and pockets deep.'

'I need to get some money,
So that I can pay my fare,
It's not a homing pigeon,
Cos it won't stay in the air.'

I said if it was a parrot,
I'd buy it and make it talk,
But no, it's a bloody pigeon,
And you can bloody walk.

Talking about animals, I might as well mention the 2 legged variety that we seem to attract and are hell-bent on vandalising the vehicles and hurling abuse at the drivers. The majority of drivers will have their own stories of bottles and bricks being thrown or kids jumping around on the bus annoying other passengers, swearing and being totally out of order. Sometimes it can be quite amusing, another driver, Chris, told me that one winter when we had a lot of snow the kids rolled large snowballs and covered Walker Road with them so buses and cars could not get past. When anybody got out to try and move them, they were pelted with snowballs. Annoying at the time but when you look back it's quite funny. On a more serious note the missiles thrown at the buses can result in someone getting injured and gave me an idea for this poem.

The Brick

Johnny and his mates were bored,
They didn't know just what to do,
They hung around bus stops and shops,
Looking for something new.

'I know!' said one of the lads,
And this will cause a fuss,
Let's all get a stone and throw them,
At the next available bus.'

So they all put a stone in their pocket,
But Johnny he chose half a brick,
They threw them at the next bus that came,
And legged it away double-quick.

'Did you see that?' laughed one of the lads,
'All of them windows we smashed,
The driver nearly had a heart attack,
It's a wonder that he didn't crash.'

Meanwhile, at the bus, an ambulance was called,
An old lady was hit by the brick,
The blood that came from the gash in her head,
Made the other passengers sick.

The lads decided to go home,
But as Johnny was going in the gate,
His mother came rushing out the door,
She looked in a bit of a state,

'C'mon John let's go to the hospital,
Your Grandma's been hit by a brick,
While she was travelling home on the bus,'
Johnny's face went white, he felt sick.

There have been a lot of changes over the years we now have assault screens, panic buttons, CCTV, Automatic Vehicle Locator (AVL), and Green Road and courses where scenarios are discussed. The assault screens while they do give a bit of protection can sometimes block vision and also make it hard to hear what people are saying, CCTV cameras were introduced to help drivers but are the first things to be looked at to show what you are doing wrong as the driver. AVL is probably one of the better things to share the location of your vehicle and Green Road monitors your driving. Now, I've been driving more than 40 years, do I need a machine to tell me how?

I was once the victim of an assault on the bus before the screens were fitted. It wasn't too bad but I suffered a bloody nose when a young lad decided to throw a punch at me in the cab. The best part was when a police officer arrived and asked me, 'Did you get his name and address?' I just looked and said, 'Excuse me, sir, will you stop hitting me and give me your name and address?' needless to say the policeman wasn't amused.

Over the years I have had a few dealings with the police a couple of speeding tickets and one for not being in control of the vehicle (I glanced at the time board). I know they are only doing their job but sometimes I think they could use a bit more discretion. Years ago the local council got sick of the parking on Barrack Road on match days so they made it a clearway. The next home game when everyone had parked and the match had started the traffic wardens went up Barrack Road and put a ticket on every car, grrr. A couple of months later I was going into town down Barrack Road and you couldn't get near any of the bus stops for all the buses belonging to the visiting fans so I stopped in the outside lane to drop off passengers who were going to the match, there was a knock on my window and a large police officer told me I couldn't stop there to which I told him I couldn't get near any of the bus stops because of the buses they had allowed to park on a clearway. He told me in an expletive manner to move, by then I was free of passengers so I did. Barrack Road remains, to this day, a glorified bus park on match days.

Chapter 7

The Millenium

As the years rolled on we soon came to the millennium, the year 2000, and throughout the world, we celebrated its arrival. On that New Year's Eve, the buses ran until the early hours of the morning, volunteers only were well paid. Although I had a bit of a reputation for doing overtime I didn't work it, wanting to spend the time celebrating with family.

Things were going quite well for me as I moved house to the one I am living in today, just around the corner from where we'd lived previously. A couple of years later, on the 13th of September 2003, my son Christopher got married to Donna. At the time we told them to enjoy themselves as we were in no hurry to be grandparents but just over a year later on the 27th of December 2004, along came our first grandchild, Kai to be followed a couple of years later by his sister, Abbie and a few years after that, another little girl, Evie and that was their family complete.

The biggest change I can remember happening was in 2005 when the licensing laws were relaxed. We went from 10.30 pm last orders and 10.45 pm closing time to pubs being allowed to open all day and into the early hours of the morning. This changed things dramatically.

Beforehand we were busy at weekends, especially Friday and Saturday, taking people into town around 7 pm, then buses going through the city centre after 10.45 pm were so busy you couldn't pick potential passengers up and had to go passed stops because you were so full. There was also quite often trouble on the buses with some people being so drunk and wanting a fight.

When the licensing laws changed it went from being overfull and trouble to hardly anybody on the bus at 11 pm. We didn't get the full bus loads of people going into town from 6.30 to 7 pm and no crowds waiting for the last buses to go home. What you did get was lots of young people catching the bus into town at about 10 pm, staying till about 2 am then getting taxis home.

My youngest son would get me to drop him off at a friend's house where they would have a few drinks, and get taxis to town at about 9.30 pm and near Christmas when he couldn't get a taxi home, I would get a phone call about 2.30 am asking me to pick him up.

Other things changed around that time as a result of the law changes. Because people were not getting off the last bus, chip shops were not getting the custom and as a result, started to close earlier. We started to get all sorts of rubbish left on the bus late at night; pizza boxes, half-full kebabs strewn across the floor as well as the normal things like lager cans and bottles rolling around.

In 2007 we were looking for a special holiday to celebrate our 30th wedding anniversary but as Linda did not like flying we were struggling to think of somewhere when Linda's mam came up with the idea of a cruise. We thought they were for old people, I was only 51 and our young son Jordan was 12 but we booked it and went and had the most fabulous time. Since then we have continued with more, albeit expensive, they are worth every penny.

In 2010 I was approached by the then-duty officer Steve Featherstone and asked if I would transfer to the Stockton depot, for a month or two. Chris Sillence, another driver, and I went to Stockton every day for about 3 months. I enjoyed the change, we were guaranteed 8 hours of pay and 4 hours of travelling time every day and as we both went in Chris' car we got shifts that finished within half an hour of each other, so as well as a change we were well paid for it.

On one occasion I was travelling through Middlesbrough when a radio message was broadcast asking me to divert because of an accident. I panicked as I didn't have a clue about the diversion but I noticed Chris coming in the other direction and as he had worked here a couple of times before I figured he would be able to tell me. I flagged him down and asked him, he just said, 'Do you not know where it is?' followed by, 'Well I'm not telling you,' and drove away laughing. Luckily I went to the bus station and got the information I needed there. I had some good laughs working at Stockton and it gave me a taste for working away so when the 2012 Olympics happened in London I immediately applied to work as a driver down there.

There were lots of drivers working at the Olympics, I was selected to go to the Paralympics just after the main games. The drivers who went to the main events stayed on a cruise ship on the Thames, lucky buggers, but we were put up in student accommodation in Bethnal Green. I can't complain, it was nice with a pub, The Salmon and Ball, about 100 yards away, which got well used and a tube station beside the pub so we never had to travel too far. We were supplied with Oyster cards enabling us to travel to the West Ham depot for work, it was great, we spent a lot of our free time travelling into central London sightseeing. I also took a couple of journeys up to relatives in Ilford.

After the initial period of 'route learning' in specially adapted vehicles designed to take 6 wheelchairs we set about picking up the wheelchair rugby teams and transporting them to training venues along the road at Leyton. The days consisted of starting early at about 6 am and after a couple of hours we checked the buses, drove them to the Hub and when given the word that our team was ready, we would go to the Olympic village in 3 buses, drop them off in Leyton and park up for a couple of hours until they were ready to go back. We would take them back to the Olympic Village drop them off again and go back to the Hub where the inspectors would tell us to take the bus back to the depot and the rest of the day was ours. It was only about 3 pm by this time and my wife called it my holiday, to be honest, she was almost right I thoroughly enjoyed it.

One of the things I enjoyed was the opportunity to watch the teams training. We asked if we could go in to watch them after taking the teams the first time and I have to admit we were in total admiration of the wheelchair athletes, and yes I mean athletes. They were fantastic whizzing down the courts throwing the ball to each other, they put a lot of able-bodied, so-called professionals to shame. On a couple of occasions, I drove the Great Britain team, one young lad had a large spiky Mohican hairstyle which was red, white and blue. They were all good lads and on one of the training sessions, they asked if we could shout and cheer like any normal crowd and we were only too happy to oblige, screaming and shouting encouragement till our voices were hoarse.

It wasn't just the British team we watched I drove the Belgium team a couple of times, I remember the Americans and their coach who was a big fellow with a long red, white and blue beard. What a nice bloke he was, I can't remember a single person who wasn't and it all added to the great friendly atmosphere that was the 2012 Olympic Games.

But alas all good things come to an end and when the games finished, because we drove the adapted buses, we were asked to stay and take them to the airport.

After being shown the route through London to Heathrow, passed all the sights in central London on the way; Houses of Parliament, Buckingham Palace, and more, and eventually onto the A4 to Heathrow we were ready to transport them to the airport on the Monday. What they also told us was that a parade was planned and some of the roads would be closed but not to worry as that wouldn't be happening until the afternoon so we would be ok. How wrong.

When Monday came, we got up very early, got the buses ready and made our way to the Olympic Village. I was assigned the Canadian team, whom we picked up about 7 am. I was following a driver from Walkergate called Cookie and was very glad because he had been driving Heathrow a lot throughout the Olympics and knew all the routes there, which was handy for what happened next.

As we left the Olympic Village and made our way into central London some of the roads were already closed. After a quick circle of Parliament Square Cookie took us along the Chelsea embankment and through streets I had never seen before. It was just as well that he knew where he was going, as I didn't have a clue and just prayed I didn't lose him.

We got to the airport, disembarked our passengers and started to make our way back. By then Cookie was long gone and I was on my own. On reaching central London again, I drove around in circles trying to find a way back to West Ham depot but I was lost. On my second trip past a police station I noticed two policemen coming out so decided to ask for directions,

'Excuse me lads I'm lost, can you help me find a way back to embankment please?'

To which came the reply, 'By that accent son, you're well lost,' and so after a bit of a laugh he proceeded to guide me back to Westminster bridge as I knew the way from there.

The next day on Tuesday, we made our way home on the Megabus from Victoria bus station and so ended my stint, or holiday, in London.

The London Olympics, 2012

The London Olympics, 2012,
A good time was had by all,
We had student digs in Bethnal Green,
Near a pub called the Salmon and Ball.

I have to admit we spent time there,
A couple of pints was all we had,
It would have been wrong to have any more,
And turn up the next day feeling bad.

After a short time of route learning,
With six wheelchairs on the bus,
We took them to a place to train,
There was always about three of us.

We watched them train and have to admit,
It made us feel rather humble,
Their disabilities didn't stop them at all,
Yet we just seem to grumble.

I had a great time in that there London,
The wife said it was a holiday.
I enjoyed what we did, made lots of friends,
And for three weeks we got decent pay.

The only downside when we got the tube,
It was like a morgue, where nobody spoke,
Even when one of the lads started to sing,
He was daft as a brush, cracking bloke.

Alas my three weeks came to an end,
The last job, a journey to Heathrow,
So I picked up a few of the Canadian team,
And along the A4 we did go.

But on the way back they shut some of the roads,
And I'm afraid I found to my cost,
I saw two policemen, and asked for directions,
Because I was totally lost.

They had a good laugh at the sound of my accent,
Said they couldn't understand why,
Then they showed me the way, bet that made their day,
And off to West Ham I did fly.

Next day got the tube to Victoria Station,
And away home on the Megabus,
The end of our time at the Paralympics,
We'd had a great time, all of us.

Two years later the Commonwealth Games were held in Glasgow and I applied to go there. *Why not? I had enjoyed London so this wouldn't be too different would it?*

Yes, it was.

There weren't as many drivers who went to Glasgow. We met at Central Station and made our way to Edinburgh then across to Glasgow to be met by someone who didn't seem to know what was going on. After a few phone calls, they put us in taxis back to Herriot Wat University just outside of Edinburgh where we were staying for the duration. Every day for the first week we were transported to the First Bus depot in Glasgow where we didn't do a lot except drive a staff bus around the same route most of the time. While at this depot we always finished about 4 pm before being taken back to our student accommodation. We found a pub just along the road for meals and more.

While there one of our group, a lad called Alan, asked the barman for a hat that was being used as a drink promotion. After he obtained the hat, he got a plastic ball with a bit of string coming out of it with BOMB written on the side. We just laughed wondering what he was going to do with it until he revealed that he was taking it to the First Bus depot with him.

We were horrified, as when we went into the depot we were searched and scanned by the Strathclyde Police who we didn't think would find it very funny. Alan later told us they were okay about it, but I'm not so sure.

Not long after, we were moved to a depot in Cumbernauld where we were eventually shown what we would be doing for the remainder of our stay in Glasgow—taking spectators to venues around the city.

I was given a new group of lads to show the routes for a couple of days, one particular route involved having to keep to the right at a junction otherwise you would get lost in Glasgow. I made sure I kept everyone informed of this, then when training had finished I was given that route up to Buchanan Bus Station. *Guess what?* I went the wrong way and got stuck, but as it was just around the corner from the bus station everyone got off and walked. I got off the bus and walked a few yards up the street where I realised I could make my way safely back. I did so and said nothing.

On another occasion I was taking a bus full of people to Hamden Park when I got a puncture so pulling off the motorway at a place called Rutherglen I was contacting the depot when a police car pulled up behind me. After seeing what was wrong, he told everyone that Hamden was just a 5-minute walk along the road, so off they all went. I couldn't believe it as I knew it took at least 5-10 minutes on the bus. Later on, when we were waiting to take people back, one gentleman informed me that he wasn't getting my bus because it took him nearly an hour to walk it, oops! Speaking to the two policemen wasn't a problem but when the tow truck came and the young mechanic was talking to the police I was left lost as to what was being said, it was pure Glaswegian.

I enjoyed my time in Glasgow and made some good friends whom I keep in touch with and meet up with occasionally, however, nothing can compare to my time at the London Olympics, my holiday, as the wife continues to remind me.

Recently a lot of drivers went to Birmingham but I thought I would give it a miss. My days of working away are over. I enjoyed them all, but I'm a home bird now.

Revisiting things that Newcastle City Council decided to change, there were significant changes John Dobson Street around this time. In my opinion, it's an expensive mistake to have halved the road making one side a cycle lane/skateboard park. It prompted me to write this poem.

White Elephant

I've lived in Newcastle all my life,
And seen some sights it's true,
But I've come to a conclusion,
The toons become a zoo.

The big market at the weekend,
Lads behave like Chimpanzees,
Climbing poles and roofs and shelters,
As if they're climbing trees.

Girls screech and point and giggle,
Whilst falling out of cars,
Like over-excited Hyenas,
Queueing for the bars.

Dressed to kill they scan the crowds,
Looking for new fellas,
Kept in line by bouncers,
In dark coats, they're like Gorillas.

And up inside St James's Park,
Wolves play with a ball,
I've even seen the Animals,
Inside the City Hall.

There's a Black Bull near the Barracks,
And Zebras cross the road,
While Cranes are helping workers,
Pick up their heavy load.

The best I've seen is John Dobson Street,
City planners hail triumphant,
A cycle lane that cost a lot,
To me, a big White Elephant.

Chapter 8

Doom and Gloom

A few years ago the driving examiner from Sunderland sent a memo through to every depot stating that he had observed drivers continually driving with only one hand and it had to stop as it is not professional and could result in an accident as you do not have full control of the vehicle. It prompted me to come up with this poem which I hope you like.

Dear Mr Carr

Dear Mr Carr,
Re your letter on the wall,
About driving with both hands,
And this applies to all.

How are you meant to pick your nose?
Scratch your arse, or even eat?
And if you feel uncomfortable,
Adjust the bloody seat?

How do you give the thumbs up,
When someone lets you out?
Or tell another driver,
When chekkies are about.

I even asked the union,
If to them this rule applied,
The answer was no comment,
On this our hands are tied.

I know it's meant for safety,
But what you don't appreciate,
Is with traffic, times and passengers,
We're always running late.

If you're wondering why I'm writing this,
Or even how and when,
It was this morning at a bus stop,
With BOTH HANDS on the pen.

Since 2020 we have struggled through the global pandemic of COVID-19. It took its toll on every country and industry, people getting vaccinated and later boosters to top up the immune system. Lots of mask-wearing, which continues today, and a lot of lives lost. People not being able to visit loved ones in care homes or attend funerals, which resulted in anger at the government for the way things were being handled. In some cases, it was justified. Since it all calmed down, 2 to 3 years later, we have been left with shortages of staff in every industry, including transport, and that has affected the mood of a lot of people.

Doom And Gloom

To all the moaners at the depot,
The Arbiters of Gloom,
Be grateful you're not an Afgan,
With their impending doom.

We complain about the wage rise,
How can you tell the wife,
While over in Afghanistan,
They're clinging on to life.

Now we've had a gripe at Brexit,
And Covid-19 hasn't gone,
If we get another lockdown,
Call it Covid 21!

We've blamed the loss of drivers,
On everything it may seem,
They've gone to pastures new,
Where the grass is always green.

So stop spreading doom and gloom,
Have a laugh and share a jest,
Make this depot great again,
Forget about the rest.

Now I'm not a cockney rebel,
And I have been here a while,
So like Clint did say, make my day,
Come up and see me, make me smile.

I had a lot of free time on my hands during this period,
it was a perfect excuse to write more poems. . .

Is There Such A Thing?

Is there such a thing as Covid?
Or is it just a plan,
By all the governments of the world,
To control their fellow man?

Tell the people it started in China,
See how much they will believe,
Feed them scientific rubbish,
They'll take it in they're so naive.

Anyone not take it seriously,
Will come down with a bump.
It's already worked in America,
We got rid of Donald Trump.

So why are kids going back to school,
Yet shutting restaurants and bars,
Is there anywhere I can escape to?
Is there really life on Mars?

If there is, they won't have covid,
Or any other daft disease,
And even on the moon,
After all, it's made of cheese...
...*Isn't it?*

Chapter 9

Barry Collins

My poems have not gone unnoticed and a couple of times I have been asked to write one for relatives, for which I obliged and have been told they liked them and were very grateful.

There is another driver at the depot, Barry Collins, who has written one or two which I think are very good and he has given permission to include them.

Dream On

I drove a bus the other day,
It was practically perfect in every way,
Believe me folks, you really must,
When I say there were no signs of rust.

I won't labour the point in this epistle,
But the steering wheel was clean as a whistle,
The heater, a marvel to behold,
Kept me warm and cosy, banished the cold.

And potholes? Not even worth a mention,
Because of the superb suspension,
It rained like Billy-oh, so to speak,
But hey, the cab, it did not leak.

I took roundabouts with no frustration,
Wow! Just feel that acceleration,
The passengers, joyous in their praise,
Were courteous and polite. Oh, happy days!

Alas, the reality was hard to take,
When from my sleep I did awake,
Twas all a dream and that hit me hard,
Now where did I put that defect card?

We once had a young lady, Val, who took it upon herself to rearrange the furniture in the locker room, and that's when Barry Collins came up with this one.

Post-War Thoughts From The Sofa

I'm just a little sofa,
Not one to cause a stink,
But I've been moved from pillar to post,
So here is what I think. . .

My position in the locker room,
Was very much debated,
I'll do my best to help you rest,
Wherever I'm located.

I'm old and creased and somewhat worn,
Understandable I guess,
It does seem like a long time,
Since my days at SCS.

So move me hither and move me thither,
It matters not one jot,
I'll still provide a comfy place,
To park your weary bot.

The End *(or maybe not. . .)*

And a final poem from Barry Collins...

Pull The Udder One

The hour was late,
And Daisy the cow,
Thought, this is the moment,
My time is now.

You think I can't do it?
Just watch me mate,
And she strolled nonchalantly,
Out of the gate.

The rest of the herd,
Looked on ... amazed,
As Daisy settled herself ...
And grazed.

This is great, thought Daisy,
As she chewed the cud,
I'm enjoying my freedom,
As any girl would.

But I know what you're thinking,
Hey what's the big deal?
Well, how would you like to be . . .
In a Happy Meal?

She dreamed of fame,
A whirlwind tour,
Before being whisked back,
To the town moor.

Which just goes to prove,
That when your dreams have died,
The grass isn't always greener,
On the other side.

I think they're all very good and I'm glad it's not just me writing and sharing them. As long as they are not of the type that nearly resulted in me losing my job, which happened when someone put a foul and sexually explicit one on the wall, and I got the blame. That took some detective work to prove my innocence.

Chapter 10

The Pen is Mightier than the Sword

In 2020 we were hit with covid a global pandemic, ordered by the government to stay in, wear masks get vaccinated etc it hit the whole country hard the majority of people worked from home the transport system was empty and no one travelled services were reduced drivers were given time off all at the government's expense this went on for nearly 2 years, it very slowly got back to near normal but even to this day you have to wear a mask in some places and some people continue to wear them.

Covid 2020

In the year of 2020,
It should have been a year of plenty.

But what we got was covid disease,
You're terrified to cough or sneeze.

In the spring that same year,
Men would cry a thousand tears.

The government pushing for electric cars,
But what they did was shut the bars.

They locked us down then overnight,
Some people said. 'Who gives a shite?'

I'm well stocked up and if it takes its toll,
I've got a hundred toilet rolls.

Then in the summer, it started to ease,
They said, 'Go out, if you please,'

But keep your space don't make a fuss,
And wear a mask when on the bus.

So we went out, we ate and drank,
And we had the government to thank.

But then, guess what? Infections grew,
Here we go, lockdown two.

Now with Christmas approaching fast,
Keep asking, 'How long can this last?'

With the vaccine hope, the Covid's gone,
All by spring in 21.

Life on the buses has been good to me. I've enjoyed most of my time here and made lots of friends both on the job and members of the public whom I got to know over the years. I still get ideas for poems which keep the mind active and as I said earlier, some people have requested me to write them for friends or relatives, for which I'm only too happy to oblige.

I have on a couple of occasions sent poems to the local newspaper one in particular that I sent in was a bit of an anti-war thing based on an idea from a book I read, The Pen Is Mightier Than The Sword by Jeffrey Archer, it has nothing to do with my time on the job but its one of my favourites.

The Pen Is Mightier Than The Sword

A leader of a country sits in his office,
His opposite leader the same,
Signing treaties of war,
Though god knows what for,
Over land to which both have a claim.

For the pen is mightier than the sword,
Here is just one reason why,
With the stroke of a pen,
Thousands of men,
Are sent out in the fields to die.

Lonely children are left without fathers,
And mothers to grieve for their sons,
Casualties of war,
Fear the knock at the door,
To tell them they've lost one so young.

Yes, the pen is mightier than the sword,
A sentence that just makes you think,
When the people in power,
Come to their final hour,
Will their hearts be blackened with ink?

As the years have rolled on Linda and I have become grandparents to four lovely children three to Christopher and Donna; Kai, Abbie and Evie and one to Jordan and Gemma, a little boy called Jenson. We are settled in our home and looking forward to enjoying retirement which isn't too far away now.

Well now we're into 2023 a lot has happened since January 1974 so I hope I remembered it all well at least all the good bits I have enjoyed putting it down on paper and for anyone who reads it to have the same enjoyment I'll sign off the way I always do,

BAZ

Printed in Great Britain
by Amazon